JOB SEARCH STRATEGIES FOR NEW GRADS

Methods that work in any Economy

ANN RAJARAM

For career advice, follow the author on her website www.greatnewreads.com or read more articles on Medium.com https://medium.com/@anupamaprv

This book is dedicated to my mom, Dr. Latha Venkataraman, for being my mentor and cheerleader. Thank you for inspiring me to reach for the stars!

Table of Contents

SECTION A – INTRODUCTION

Ch 1. INTRODUCTION

Congratulations!

If you recently graduated, then congratulations on making it through college. I am sure you are thrilled about joining the "Adult" world, with real jobs and salaries and the exciting lure of all the wonderful things money can buy!

If you are still in college, and bought this book to land a decent internship, then kudos to you too! You are obviously quite proactive, and this "hustle" mentality will take you far in life! Good job!

With those initial pleasantries, let us get started. I know you are rearing to go and want to land your dream job or internship as quickly as possible. This chapter will outline the basic steps so you can optimize your time and efforts, land a lucrative and meaningful role, and get started with the next phase of life!

Some of the steps might feel counter-intuitive, some might feel unnecessary, but believe me – all are mandatory! Just as sharpening a saw reduces the actual cutting time, the preparatory steps in this book will help you speed up your job search process and improve the odds of landing a fabulous job opportunity.

Without further ado, let us get started…

1.1 Job Search during Covid19.

A special note in light of this pandemic. I graduated in 2008 – at the peak of a global recession. Jobs were scarce, salaries plummeted, confirmed job offers were rescinded or delayed. Instead of competing for jobs with classmates, our graduating class was competing with thousands of experienced hires who were also looking for work. It WAS gloomy.

Things are similar with Covid19. However, I want to assure you that things will get better; this too shall pass. Moreover, if you follow the steps in this book, you can accelerate your job search faster than conventional methods.

1.2 What is in this Book?

Many people will tell you that looking for a decent job, especially in today's weak economy, is a job into itself. Applicants can spend weeks and months learning "marketable" skills, apply to hundreds of jobs online and… SILENCE.

- So where are the good jobs? How do you get started?
- How do you land one quickly?
- What if you have a geographic preference or want to pivot to a role that is only tangentially related to your degree or major?

This book aims to answer these burning questions and help you land a full-time well-paying job quickly (preferably in under 90 days). This books cuts through the generic resume advice and gives practical advice on where the best jobs are, and how to get to an interview stage.

Over the last few years, I have advised and successfully helped dozens of friends, relatives and friend-of-friends land a lucrative job in the data science field, even though I am NOT a recruiter. I have formally mentored folks at work and outside, so realized many of these tips translate well to almost all tech jobs and work for most new grads.

So, I can vouch that these tips work!

1.3 Audience for this Book

1.3.a WHO should read this book?

- If you have spent countless hours applying to dozens of jobs online and have received zero or no job offers.
- Women, looking for work after a career break, including spouses on H-4 or L2 EAD (Employee Authorization, a type of work visa issued in the US).
- Students (including F-1/ OPT visa international students) close to graduation who are eager to get a job.
- You have a child, husband or other close relative who is struggling to get a job after graduation (undergrad or masters) and would like to help.

1.3.b Who should NOT start this book?

- If you are looking for a role specific to the field of Data Science (data engineer, data scientist, data visualization analyst or similar) then please look at my other book "Data Science Jobs" also available on Amazon. In addition to job search methods, that book has specific guidance on technical interview questions on a variety of topics like R/Python programming, Tableau, machine learning algorithms as well as ideas and tutorial resources for building your project portfolio.

- If you desperately need a job and/or money in the next week, then put down this book and look elsewhere. Even if I set you up for an interview tomorrow, (and no one can do it so fast) the hiring process in most companies is at least a month long. Most people take 2 to 3 months to get hired. 30 days is the minimum lead time for this book to work.
- You are not willing to tailor your resume, work on the strategies in this book or put in the hours to make your profile look irresistible to hiring managers.
- You only believe books with 100,000 words or longer. Job searchers do not need a thesis, they need quick actionable items to help them get started in their career. This book is deliberately kept short and concise with no fluff. This will help you read quickly and get ahead in your job search.

1.4 New Grad Starter Questions

1.4.a I am just exploring / looking to get started?

If you are just exploring roles and do not intend to start working in the next 6 months, then this book will guide you on how to strengthen your resume for the future.

- Start with section A for an overview about the field.
- Read chapters 2 and 3 from section B. Do not jump ahead until you have mastered the prerequisite coding skills!

- Read chapter 4 from section C. This will help you optimize your project portfolio and create a custom learning path that is best suited for your previous skills and experience and your expectations for a job.
- Once you start applying for jobs, read section D, which includes behavioral Qs and interview procedures.

1.4.b I completed a course/ I just graduated/ I am already applying for jobs

If you are already in the job search stage, then please follow the sequence below. Yes, I understand that some of you are close to graduation or desperately seeking a job ASAP. However, the time spent in honing your resume for keywords and creating a stellar online profile will reap tremendous benefits in the long run, even if it feels futile or time-consuming in the short run.

Please, follow the steps IN SEQUENCE, without skipping any parts:

- Skim Section A.
- Read chapter 2 in section B. If your profile is missing key skills, you will face an uphill battle convincing any employer that you are an asset. Please make sure you have all the required skills. If yes, move on to section C. If not, please refer to the learning resources to learn them in parallel with your job search.
- Skim Section D to make sure you are aware of all the possible interview stages, so you can prepare well.

- Read Section C thoroughly to make appropriate changes to your profile. Some strategies may seem counter-intuitive or even too simple, but these work 100%.
  - Chapter 9 on Upwork will help you start earning immediately.
  - Chapter 6 and 7 will help you find leads that you have most likely overlooked.
  - The other chapters in this section will be beneficial in casting a wide net as possible. After all, you just need one confirmed job offer to get started!

1.5 Book Layout

The summary below gives you an idea of what to expect in the coming chapters:

1.5.a Section B – Learning and Skill building

- ***How to gain in-Demand Skills that get you Hired*** –High level learning plan to establish yourself in your field.
- ***Resources for Technical Skills*** best websites and reputed links where you can learn programming skills for advancing your career.

1.5.b Section C - Job Search Help

- ***Profiles that get hired*** – please, do not skip this chapter. If your online profile and resumes are truly stellar, this chapter will validate it. If not, the tips will help you get hired faster.
- ***Where are the jobs?*** - Baltimore is full of healthcare analytics; Calgary caters to oil industry

and streaming analytics, while Detroit is full of startups. Different locations and industries have slightly different job requirements. Knowing these can help you mount a targeted campaign, or at least set more realistic expectations.

- *LinkedIn* - This chapter focuses solely on LinkedIn, with strategies other than hitting the default "Apply" button.
- *Twitter* – This site is rarely used as a job-hunt resource, which is why you can steal a march over other jobseekers.
- *Networking* – Nothing beats old-fashioned connections. This chapter will help you identify and leverage connections that you did not know existed and meet with the folks who can get you hired.
- *Upwork* – Build your portfolio and start earning within a week. Most people fail to utilize Upwork and are disappointed when they do not make any money. This chapter will give you the correct tips to start earning on this wonderful platform.
- *Good Old Search* – This chapter lists many niche sites, and websites with job postings. Apply the tips you learned in the previous chapters to make the most of these sites.

1.5.c Section D - Interview Preparation

- *Interview Process*
- *Interview Qs*
- *Some more advice* – For more Qs and topics not covered in other chapters.

Final disclaimer, all the strategies in this book have been tested successfully for dozens of folks, but only in the US and India. This proves these principles are suitable for multiple job markets, but not necessarily all markets. There are exclusions to every rule, so please do not consider this book to be legal advice, and tweak accordingly.

1.6 Basic Job Search Action Plan

Assuming you already have the technical chops, this is the basic approach you will follow:

- **Action #1** - Read chapters 4 and 5, i.e. "profiles that get hired" and "where are the jobs" to polish your resume and profile. If you need to start earning or show employment (F-1 students, for example) then navigate to the chapter on Upwork.
- **Action #2** – Start with LinkedIn to apply to the jobs with the best chance of getting hired.
- **Action #3** – Work on the job search strategies using the chapters on Twitter, search, networking. LinkedIn is still the largest marketplace for jobs, but the others are good supplements, to increase your chances.

1.7 How long will it take me to get a job?

Nothing in this life is guaranteed, especially not a job. The market could crash tomorrow and hiring freezes could impede your goals. An old friend could decide to return a favor and hire you tomorrow!

However, assuming nothing major changes in your life and the economy, and you have the necessary skills, we will assign 1 week for tasks related to polishing your profile itself and the job research. Actual job matching using LinkedIn and Twitter with the strategies listed in this book will last 2-4 weeks. Ideally, you should start receiving feedback from recruiters and managers in 10 days or so. The hiring processes in most companies take at least 4 weeks, to receive an offer letter, starting from the day you receive an HR or introductory call.

Assuming you will do your personal branding and social media postings in parallel, most folks have seen results in 2-3 months.

1.8 Mothers returning to work

It is sad that brilliant women are penalized for taking care of young kids. My personal peeves aside, this is what DID work for mothers I know, irrespective of the years in their career break:

- The first job will be hardest to get, so do not give up hope easily. Most women will find a job in under 4 months.
- The first job is the hardest to find! So, you may have to compromise and accept the first role you get, preferably at a small firm. Do not fret, if you do a great job you will get promoted or receive a jump in pay. If not, stay 6 months and then move on to better roles. The starting pay might not be what you expect, but it is still better than no salary at all.

- Startups are great too, as you can learn multiple skills and then jump couple of levels at your next gig. Just ensure you are not expected to do tons of overtime without compensation.
- Remember the skills that helped you be a super mom, wife and homemaker will also help you shine once you land that first job.
- Look for women-only hiring events. Many large employers hold annual events to increase diversity in tech. Ask around in your friend and family circle and look for local event news.

1.9 Bonus Content

Please note that I will be periodically be updating this book with bonus content based on changes in the market, new hiring trends, frequently asked questions and more. So, remember to check back into this book for new content, tips, and strategies. All bonus material will be added to chapter 14 – "bonus content".

Without further ado, let us get started…

SECTION B – LEARNING & SKILL BUILDING

Ch 2. BASIC LEARNING RESOURCES

You have just completed your degree and breathed a sigh of relief that you are done with reading, assignments and all the "boring" learning stuff.

WRONG!

Success requires continuous learning. This is a knowledge economy and if you do not keep track of advances in your field and picking new skills, you will be left behind! College is a great platform for building basic life skills, and teaches you "how to learn", but you do need to keep building on that solid foundation.

Some of you might also realize that your majors are decent, but the jobs you are applying to, all require skillsets that you have never worked on. Do not worry, there are many sites where you can pick up a working knowledge of those skills for free or low prices. This chapter lists some of those sites. Once you land a job, your employer might have access to other pricier sites, so do take advantage if you get a chance! Either way, managers love folks who proactively improve their skills outside company time and are happy to promote such star employees.

The sections below will tell you some free and low-cost sites where you can pick up new skills without breaking the bank. I have personally used/reviewed all the sites and courses in this chapter, so I can vouch for these recommendations.

2.1 Communication

Communication, both verbal and written, is an essential skill if you want to get ahead at work. Being able to persuade others and presenting well in a tangible skill that will help you in every domain.

To improve speaking skills, think about presenting at local meetups or in office or even joining a Toastmaster's club.

To improve writing skills consider starting a blog or posting to Medium.com. You do not need to earn money, but the views and traffic shows whether you can write in a compelling fashion or not.

2.2 Specific Coding Skills

2.2.a Excel VBA

Irrespective of your domain, having some coding proficiency is a particularly useful skill to possess and improves your value to your employer and clients. If you are unsure where to start and have zero coding experience, start with Excel/VBA. Almost everyone uses Excel, especially reports seen by senior executives and C-suite folks, so try to go beyond power pivot and learn how to program macros. This will allow you to automate mundane jobs and free up time and earn brownie points for "coding". As a side note, the latest versions of Excel offer some amazing built-in data analysis, reporting and programming features. Go for it!

As a side bonus, learning VBA will eliminate some of the fear most people have towards programming! It is not as hard or mystical as you think it is.

Some sites to pick this up:

1. Udemy - https://www.udemy.com/course/excel-vba-and-macros-course/
2. Guru99 - https://www.guru99.com/vba-tutorial.html
3. Books – The Dummy series book is a great starting point - https://www.amazon.com/Excel-Programming-Dummies-John-Walkenbach/dp/1119077397

2.2.b Python

Although Python has recently become popular as a tool of choice for DataScience, it is a great multi-purpose programming language and quite easy to pick up. You can use it to create web applications, automate repetitive tasks and do data analysis too!

Remember you just want to learn enough to make life easy, not to become a professional software developer. My recommendation is to learn Python only if you took some basics in college, or if you already completed a course on VBA. VBA and Python are not similar, but having comfort in the former will help you gain confidence and learn Python faster.

Some sites to learn Python:

1. Python for Everybody - https://www.py4e.com/. This site is free and is the foundation for a class with the same name on Coursera. Go directly to Coursera if you need some hand holding or would like a verified certificate.

2. Udemy - https://www.udemy.com/course/the-python-mega-course/ There are tons of courses on Udemy, but this one is generic enough and the real-world projects will give you a very happy sense of accomplishment.
3. Book – Automate the boring stuff with Python by Al Sweigar. This book has real world projects, and you do not need to complete every chapter in the book. Just practice the topics that seem relevant to you. Amazon link below - https://www.amazon.com/dp/B00WJ049VU/ref=d p-kindle-redirect?_encoding=UTF8&btkr=1

2.3 Create a Website – Showcase your Portfolio

Almost every job seeker can benefit from having a portfolio. This will make you more attractive to employers as this is something tangible that they can see.

Portfolios are mandatory if you are in programming, technology or careers like graphic designers, writers, artists, etc. Even marketers, social media managers and product managers can show off their projects by creating a one-page flyer showing the brands they have worked with. Even if you do not have any big brand names or only academic projects, consider using the domain name – for example, "local fashion boutique", "art gallery", "bike shop", etc.

If you are still stumped, login to Upwork and look for job contracts. Do not bid, but just brainstorm what you would do, and create a solution.

Upwork is a fabulous site to get paid gigs you until you get hired full-time. At the same time, you can modify the same projects and add to your portfolio. Having freelancer experience on Upwork is a fabulous way of being unique and standing out to potential employers! As a recruiter once told me, "it is easier to hire someone who already has a job, than to evaluate someone who doesn't!"

You may also want to reach out to non-profits in the area and build your portfolio! Be creative.

2.4 Learning Starter Questions

2.4.a Should I go for a masters or graduate degree?

Student Debt - If you already have loads of student debt, then another degree is not the best bet, even if you see very few companies hiring for your major. The pandemic has shrunk the number of jobs available, so it will take a bit longer; do not lose hope.

There are many skills you have learnt in college that translate across industries. For example, a major in theater can help in visual arts and UX tester roles. You can easily pick up the UX wireframe software with ease.

Immigration - If you are outside the US and intend to immigrate to US/Europe/Canada, then an international degree is one way of legal immigration. However, the costs are steep, and you lose the ability to earn for 2 full years. Plus, immigration laws are getting tougher, so job competition is high. Remember to count the lost opportunity of earning as well as the risk of market saturation by the time you graduate.

Some employers are offering a partial or full educational reimbursement for tuition costs, then an additional degree is a good idea. But do an honest check whether you can truly balance the time commitments. Online degree courses are as rigorous as full-time classes and it might take you longer to graduate if you space out classes too much. Most employers also expect a reasonable grade (A or B) or else the reimbursement policies do not apply. If you have kids, or caregiver duties or other commitments, then a full-time degree commitment may feel overwhelming once the initial motivation wears off.

2.4.b No Experience – The Catch22 Situation

If you follow the subsequent chapters and apply those principles, you should be able to land a decent job.

However, if you can afford it, in the interim, work pro bono for non-profits, local merchants. Make cold calls. Apply on Upwork. Work as a freelancer.

Finding a good job is ultimately a numbers game – you only need one role to achieve success!

2.5 Apply for jobs strategically.

Please do NOT randomly apply to every single analytics job in the country. Be strategic using LinkedIn to reach out to hiring managers. Remember, it is better to hear "NO" directly from the hiring manager than to apply online and wait in eternity.

Competition is getting fierce, so be methodical. The next few chapters in this book will help you pinpoint the best jobs in your target city and connect with hiring managers for jobs that are not posted anywhere else.

If your first job is not at your dream company, do not despair. Earn and learn. Every company, big or small, will teach you valuable skills that will help you get better and snag your ideal role next year. I do recommend staying at roles for at least 12 months, before switching, otherwise you will not have anything impactful to discuss in the next interview.

2.6 Other Resources for Continuous learning.

2.6.a Conferences

Some will be pricey, but most will have discounts for students and new graduates. Choose the ones which have separate sessions for students and networking/hiring sessions. Most have become online, considering the pandemic, so you will not even incur hotel/flight costs!

2.6.b. Meetups

Do not go to meetups only for badgering for a job. Instead, consider a 50-50 split. Choose half your meetups where the sessions help you gain more insights into real-world applications, new trends in your industry, interact with folks who can offer advice.

The other half should be job fairs/ hiring events. There are more than you think you know – try checking Eventbrite site in your zip code or even a Google search.

2.7 ACTION ITEMS

- Look up the resource sites and bookmark them for the future.

- Look if there are hiring events in your area and add to your Google/Outlook calendar.
- Go to Meetup.com and check for groups that relate to your field or the industry you want to get into. Join at least 2 such groups.

SECTION C - JOB SEARCH

Ch 4. PROFILES THAT GET HIRED

No one boards an international flight without a passport and appropriate visa/travel documents. Airport security will simply bar you at the gate. Similarly, unless you showcase a "hire-worthy" profile you will be weeded out by both human and electronic application tracking systems.

4.1 What makes a stellar profile?
These are basic attributes that need to be fulfilled before any hiring manager will even look at your resume. They do not guarantee a job by themselves, but not having them is a guarantee for resume rejections!

4.1.a LinkedIn profiles:
A LinkedIn profile rated as "All-star". (see image from my profile below. This is a system generated badge that indicates your profile is completed with all relevant details. So, your name should crop up when a potential employers or recruiter searches for a suitable candidate. We will go into more details in later sections.

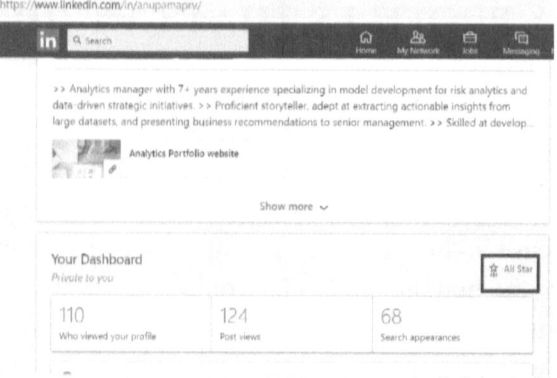

4.1.b Professional website:

If you want to work in technology or creative arts, then having a portfolio and personal website is a must.

- If you do not have one already, then please create a FREE, simple blog on WordPress and write about your learning journey.
- You might even want to look at low-cost hosting for your own domain and website via sites like WordPress, Squarespace and Wix. These can be set up within a couple of hours even if you have zero background in coding. Really, there is no excuse not to have one.
- For techies, connect your site to your GitHub profile. If you do not have one, then please do create a GitHub profile, irrespective of whether you have your own site! Many employers are now mandatorily asking for GitHub links and often ask candidates to share a code repository so they can look. Some also expect candidates to walk the manager through code from this repo, so do not wait for an employer to ask until you decide to start one. In most cases, the lack of a Github

profile might put you out of the running before you even know you were considered.

- Add links to your personal site (and GitHub, if applicable) to your LinkedIn profile.

4.1.c Hybrid resume:

A resume that highlights what you can do for potential employers in the top half of the first page. Managers are busy, and you want to make sure that your resume interests them enough for a second look. No one has time to read through even 2 pages of resume, so the first half page should scream that you fit their criteria. More on this later.

4.1.d Relevant Marketable skills:

These should be listed on your resume, your LinkedIn profile, your social media profiles, and some should also be part of your elevator pitch.

4.2 LinkedIn profiles

There are many excellent articles on what makes an amazing LinkedIn profile. A condensed version based on profile sections is listed below. All these sections must be mandatorily filled in:

4.2.a LinkedIn profile:

This is a must, where your profile and photo are visible to public. Until you get your dream job, data privacy will have to take a back seat. Sad, but true. Also fill out your experience and education details.

Profile picture must be professional. Photos give a personal connection, so they must be visible to the public. You are applying for a job in data science, not reality TV.

4.2.b Connections:

You need a fully completed LinkedIn profile with at least 500+ connections. If you just completed your undergrad, then you may be able to get away with only 300+ connections. Any less and it looks like you do not socialize well which raises suspicions that you may not be a team player. Only CEOs, billionaires, tenured professors, and senior executives get to live with an incomplete or non-existent LinkedIn profile. Reach out to all your classmates, friends, family, neighbors, import your contacts. Do what you need to; but increase your connections. This will also ensure the odds that someone in your extended network will be the hiring manager who will offer you a job. It also will help you look up relevant posts, discussed in the LinkedIn chapter 4.

4.2.c Recommendations:

Have at least 3 recommendations. If you do not have any, ask classmates, friends, or family to give you some. Write a 50-word recommendation template for them, so they do not need to think too much.

4.2.d Projects:

This is mandatory for folks in tech and creative arts. However, almost all majors can benefit from having a portfolio of projects. Think marketing, writers, fashion designers, graphic designers, architects, etc.

It is perfectly acceptable to describe academic projects or codebase you did in college or from an online course. Even better if you took it further or applied similar work to a different brand/dataset/context.

Do not copy/paste proprietary code, though.

4.2.e Skills:

Skills act as SEO keywords for your profile. For example, when someone is searching for a data scientist, then LinkedIn's algorithms include the title and relevant skill keywords (Python, Data Wrangling, Machine Learning Algorithm, Bayesian analysis, etc.) to decide who to push up the top. Each endorsement that you get for your skill helps your chances further, and endorsements for skills by experts will help you bubble up higher.

Choosing skills, however, is tricky and is different based on your target role, company, and domain. Follow the steps below to get a better idea of which skills are popular and important.

- Log in to LinkedIn and type in "<dream title> <dream company>" in the LinkedIn search bar. Select "People" if it is not selected. I have used Bloomberg as the company and "Copywriter" as an example as shown in image below:

- Look at 5 profiles who have worked at this company for at least 18 months, and then look at the skills they have listed. You will notice some skills get repeated on all the profiles or are modifications of the same thing. Make sure these skills are listed in your profile, but only if you have them. If you do not, then try to gain those skills as quickly as possible.
- Repeat for 3 target companies. If your job search has geographical constraints, then add city names in the search bar. Add skills on your profile based on your research.
- Reach out to your network and get endorsed for those skills. If your network has someone who has 20+ endorsements for that skill, then specifically request them to endorse you.
- Note, before you send out requests for endorsements, make sure those skills are listed as the first 5 skills. Otherwise folks must unnecessarily look through your 50 allowed skills and most will abandon the task. LinkedIn sorts skills based on a default order of date the skill was added, and which ones you are most endorsed for, so you will have to manually re-order your skills. This is annoying, but unfortunately necessary. [I do not have any proof this is how LinkedIn algorithms work, but the technique has worked for me, and for all the folks who made modifications following my advice]

4.2.f Headlines and summary:

LinkedIn will display your most recent job title and industry as the default headline, but that is a waste of SEO power, especially if you had a break in your career or are pivoting from another stream.

Choose a headline based on the role you are looking for, and please do not state "Actively looking" or "open to opportunities". I have heard mixed opinions on this, but unless you are a student, advertising you are unemployed and unable to get a job only seems to hurt your chances. Err on the side of caution, and do not show desperation on LinkedIn.

Use the summary tab to write a succinct description of your skills and the value you bring to the table. My current profile screenshot is listed below:

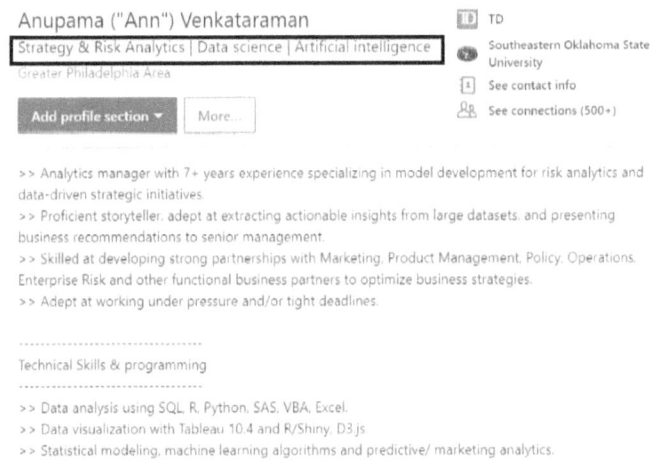

4.2.g Certifications:

LinkedIn allows you to export certificates from several online learning sites, including Udemy, Coursera, Udacity, EdX, and many others. Worst case, you can manually enter the certifications, and attach links to the image. Host images on your personal website, GitHub, or Google Drive.

These certifications act as testimonials for your skills, and as keyword matching. I once got a message from a recruiter who was looking for Hadoop expertise in the area, even though I had only learnt it in my spare time. I passed on the job, but it was interesting to know that certifications pushed me up in the search listings.

Once you have filled out all these sections, your profile should be marked as "all-star" and increase the "searchability" of your profile. Look at how your "public" profile looks to others and make changes as appropriate.

Next, the acid test – type "data analyst" (or your preferred job title) in the search bar and then filter for your location. Scroll through the names and titles of the results. If your profile is not visible in the first 5 pages, then either you are in a saturated market (San Francisco), or your profile still needs some editing, or both. If you are not in the first 5 pages, and your profile is all-star, then do not worry too much. This limits the number of searches you will feature in, so you may receiver lesser messages from hiring managers. You can overcome this point, by using the search strategies in the following chapters.

4.3 Hybrid Resumes

Resumes can be functional, chronological or hybrid. I personally prefer the "hybrid" version, as it presents the details most relevant to the job I am applying. Unless you have 10+ years of experience, the "hybrid" resume will fit your needs.

- Note, multiple recruiters and clients have hired me (and my protegees) on the strength of our "hybrid" formats. So, the format works.
- Occasionally, managers or HR personnel will come back to me asking for a chronological format. I always comply because the purpose of the resume is accomplished, i.e. getting noticed by the hiring decision-maker.
- US recruiters often expect resumes to be 2 pages or less. Mine is 4 pages, but the hybrid format ensures that I've never received any complaints. Only ton of job offers!
- Notice how the format clubs job functions together, rather than job titles. Titles and work history time frames have been relegated to the end, under work history. This deliberate format ensures managers who look at the resume read the most important details at the very beginning.
- Even if you have limited experience, you should be able to describe your academic projects using this format.
- Tweak the "objective" based on your career goals.
- Do not lie or fabricate on your resume. You will be found out!

- If you completed your LinkedIn profile adequately, you would have enough content to create such a resume.

4.4 Sample Resume

My personal resume screenshot below: (some parts truncated)

Anupama ("Ann") Puthur Venkataraman

OBJECTIVE   Proactive analytics professional looking for managerial roles where my analytics programming and consulting skills can help deliver data-driven business solutions to accelerate growth!
Excellent communication and presentation skills, from working directly with clients, senior stakeholders, vendors and multiple lines of business.

SKILLS

Programming	Tableau, R, SQL, Python, SAS, C/C++, HTML, Unix, SAP-ABAP, VBA, Advanced Excel user.
Project Management	MS Project, Clarity, JIRA, Trello, Shiny and Excel Dashboards, business reporting.
Analytics	Hadoop, Machine learning, predictive modeling, financial modeling.

FUNCTIONAL EXPERIENCE:

Data Science / Analytics

- Develop fraud monitoring models and strategies to mitigate the fraud loss while balancing customer experience, operational and product P&L impacts.
- Implement real-time rules for card transactions in TSYS, VBV (Verified by Visa) and internal decision engine.
- **Ranked Top 10%** in Kaggle competition for creating highly accurate predictive model for calculating customer satisfaction and churn for Santander Bank.
- **Scoring models** – Create segmented scoring model for cloud-based behavioral assessment tool and user profiling for mobile dating app.
- **Text and Social media analytics** - Designed and implemented Twitter analysis web-tool for in-house storage and analysis of change in Twitter Follower Counts for media client.
- Advanced analytics using machine learning algorithms (Random Forest, Classification, regression and clustering methods) and REST API programming.

- Owner and blogger at www.journeyofanalytics.com

Financial and Strategy modeling:
- Financial modeling to understand ROI from implementing fraud strategies for new product campaigns, as well as evaluating vendor scoring models.
- Use risk analysis models to identify pricing change resulting in **$30,000 increase in revenue** per month.
- Create new financial plan to improve collection strategies for urgent care clinic, for pending bills and to reduce future defaults.
- Design/maintain billing simulators for verifying updates to accounting systems based on pricing changes.

Project management:
- **Lead dashboard development** and fraud monitoring for new online authentication tool used with digital marketing campaigns.
- **Develop implementation roadmap** for cloud-based behavioral assessment tool, including cloud architecture plan, high level **database design schema, infrastructure** cost and resource planning, security considerations for enterprise client users, etc. **Work with client COO and Microsoft Azure team** for first phase of software implementation.
- Lead cross-functional team **for critical datacenter upgrade project at** BlackRock. Completed project rollout 1-month before schedule across 3 datacenters, with seamless transition and zero impact to clients.

Client Relations/ Communication Skills:
- Present results and recommendations from data analysis to senior management.
- Coordinate with BlackRock client relationship managers, internal and client-side technical teams throughout implementation cycle and maintenance SLA period.
- Technical contact for SAP functional experts (FiCo, CRM, BW modules) at Infosys.

EDUCATION
BE (Electronics), PIIT, University of Mumbai, India. (Honors)

MBA Finance, Southeastern Oklahoma State University. (in progress)

WORK HISTORY

May 2014 – Mar 2015. **Analyst**, BlackRock Inc.

Aug 2012 – Dec 2013. **Lab instructor & Teaching Assistant**, University of Delaware.

Mar 2009- Jan 2011. **Systems Engineer**, Infosys Technologies, Ltd. India (multiple offices)

CERTIFICATIONS

- Foundations of Business Strategy, Udemy.
- Credit Risk Modeling in R, DataCamp.
- Foundations of Marketing Analytics, Coursera.
- Taming Big Data with MapReduce and Hadoop, Udemy.
- Inbound marketing certification, HubSpot.
- Google Analytics Individual Qualification.
- Developing Data Products, Coursera.
- Operations Management, Udemy.

AWARDS

- Ranked Top 10% worldwide Kaggle Santander (analytics) competition.
- 1 of 10 worldwide IEEE Travel grant recipients, to attend 5-day IPS Conference at Bellevue, WA. (2013)
- Excellence award by client for Top Performance, Novartis SISNET/Infosys Pune.
- Emerging Leader certificate for completing Blue Hen Leadership Program, UD.

VOLUNTEER WORK & EXTRA-CURRICULARS:

- Women Initiative Network (WIN), Philadelphia Chapter, Nasdaq.
- Office Volunteer, DVI Materials Resource Center.
- Lab instructor, E&R department, Infosys-Pune campus.
- Co-Editor, "Gurukul" – company-wide magazine for new recruits at Infosys.

Please use this format to tweak your resume. It will take time, but it is completely worth it. If you feel you need professional help with your resume, then please consult Upwork or Fiverr for those type of services. Note, my resume is listed under the "Resources – Career

Resources" page of my website under the header "Career Guidance". My website is www.journeyofanalytics.com

Quick Favor

Did you like this book so far?

If so, please consider leaving a review. Your feedback will be beneficial to me (as an author) and other readers. You do not have to write a whole lot, just a numeric star review will do.

For some reason, if you did not find the book useful and choose to leave a 3* review or less, please do email me at ann_venkat@greatnewreads.com Your thoughts will help me improve the book for the next iteration.

Ch 5. WHERE ARE THE JOBS?

Do you know "**WHERE**" you would like your new job to be?

Unless you are married, most people do not have a valid answer for this, especially students who are close to graduation and are willing to relocate anywhere.

5.1 Why location matters

Sadly, location does matter because companies in specific industries tend to concentrate in specific cities. For example, healthcare and defense research companies in the Baltimore area while Los Angeles and New York are havens for artists, creative careers, and professionals in the entertainment world. Salary range, skill requirements and even job titles will also be different.

In large banks or fintech startups, "social media analyst" jobs could be listed under different titles like digital marketing analyst, media analyst or even "associate".

On the practical side, many managers simply do not have the budget to have candidates flown in for in-person interviews and may not be interested in paying for relocation costs.

Job market research is, therefore, crucial before you start applying.

Special Note – The pandemic has made "remote jobs" more attractive, but things will eventually open. However, for the purpose of this chapter, it is important that you think carefully about which locations you would be happy relocating.

5.2 Job Market research

The job market research in the section below will help you identify the best roles in the area and indicate if you need to expand your area of search or look for a different title.

If you are a student, with no specific favorites, pick SFO and another 2 cities like Chicago or Philadelphia. Yes, all are in different corners of the country. If you do not have a preference, then start with NYC or San Francisco, despite the high living expenses. It continues to be the largest hotbed of jobs and industries because of the concentration of companies like Google, LinkedIn, Microsoft, and a plethora of startups. Not to say it is the only city with lucrative jobs – other major cities like Charlotte (NC), Philadelphia, Baltimore, Dallas, Chicago, Detroit, Denver, and Boston also have multiple opportunities. But SFO or NYC are excellent starting points.

Now, let us start on the market research portion:

1. Open LinkedIn and navigate to the jobs section. Type "data scientist" in the keyword bar, and target location in the "city" bar. If you live in a city close to another larger city, then choose the larger city. For example, if your target city like "Wilmington, DE", then choose "greater Philadelphia" instead since we are still in the research phase and want a broad selection.

In case, you are not familiar with job search in LinkedIn, the image below indicates navigation for the jobs (1), keyword bar (2) and location search bar (3). As a sample, I am using the job role "accountant" in the Charlotte, NC area.

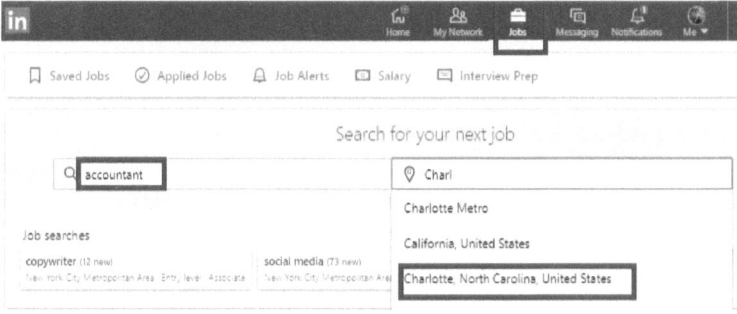

2. Once you get the initial search results, select (a) date posted tab on the top left, and then (b) choose past month.

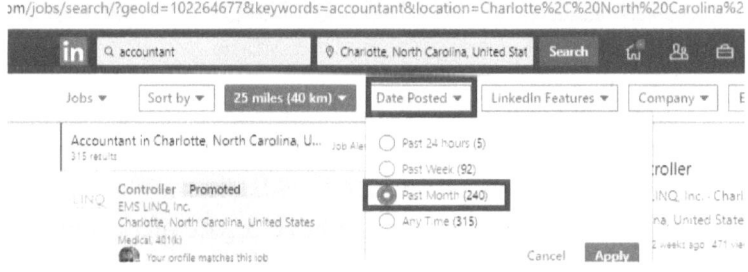

3. Note the number of results it returns and scroll down through the company names. As seen from the image below, there are 315 results for this area. I have hidden the "promoted" results. The other top results include multiple companies and even a small accounting firm.

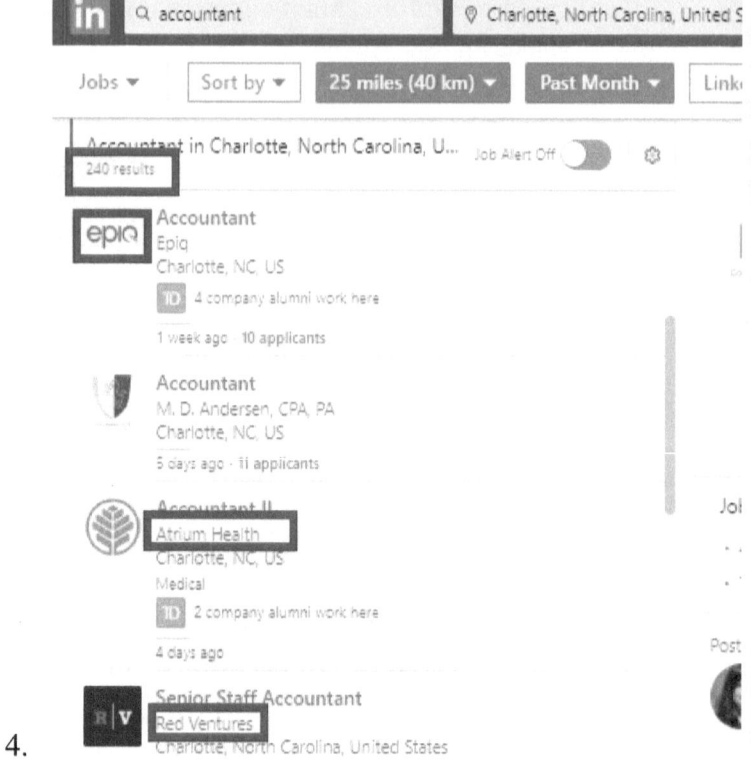

4.

5. Click on the job roles and read through the job requirements, to see patterns in skill requirements and experience requirements. If most roles need 7+ years and you only have 3, you are going to be passed over, although you may have a shot with 5 or 6 years. If the roles all call for a specific software tool, then check how you can quickly master those basics from Udemy or a library book.

6. Repeat for related terms like "payroll analyst" in the search bar, and same target geography. This will expand the search and show you roles with alternate job titles, if any. I chose "payroll analyst"

because the last result was payroll supervisor. You will also notice companies you may have not known existed in the area, or titles that pique your interest.

7. If you live in a smaller city, say Greensboro, NC, then the results will be less in number (58) and skill requirements might vary or be more/less stringent. In this case, be mindful that it will either take longer to find the right role, or you need to expand your search.

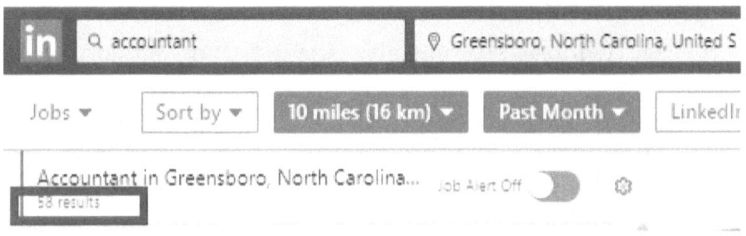

8. Use the skills from this research to update your resume and be sure to add them in the "skills" section under your LinkedIn profile. Also make note of all the job titles and companies; we will use them in the next chapters. DO NOT APPLY; not yet.
9. Repeat the same on Indeed.com and make notes of the company names, titles and skills.
10. Navigate to glassdoor.com and get the salary range. Note, living expenses differ by location, so an $80k salary in Philadelphia is worth more than $95k in SFO or Boston. If you are an experienced employee, transitioning from a different domain or role, and the salary feels like a step down, check if you would qualify for a more senior or managerial role.

11. For salary ranges, use Glassdoor.com look at the national averages first and then salary for your nearest geographic location. This will be the range you can reasonably expect. Personally, I have found Glassdoor to be remarkably accurate, compared to sites like Payscale.com or indeed.com. For readers in Canada use glassdoor.ca, glassdoor.in for India. For others, use the corresponding link for your country.

5.3 Action Items

a. Choose a target city, identify, and update profile with skills and create list of top 2 job titles for the roles in the area.

b. Recognize salary ranges for your target role in the area you expect to work.

Ch 6. LINKEDIN – CREATIVE WAYS TO STAND OUT

LinkedIn is the leader of all job search sites, and one which I have personally found the most profitable. Unfortunately, simply using the "apply" button on job postings does not work for most candidates. And if you see a button named "apply on site" then please refrain, your resume is going to end up in the cyber-world black hole called application tracking system, never to be heard again. Do not be fooled by the auto-generated acknowledgement emails from LinkedIn or the parent company.

Personally, I would rather hear "NO" from a manager than wait indefinitely with zero feedback.

Instead be strategic and use LinkedIn to connect directly with the gatekeepers and decision-makers using the strategies below.

6.1 Job posts from content tab

This is one of the best and most under-used methods of finding a great job on LinkedIn. Instead of applying to LinkedIn jobs, you will directly reach out and respond to original job posters.

Here is how you do it:

1. Remember the job titles and location you so painstakingly researched from the previous chapter? Well type them in the search bar of the

home page and choose "content". An example is shown below for data scientist Dallas.

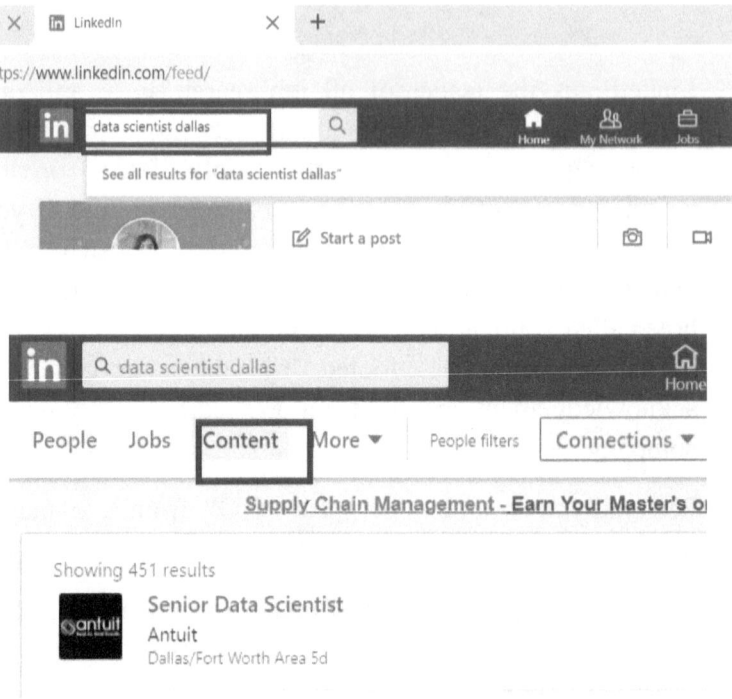

2. Once you get the results, select "past week" from the date posted dropdown options. Content posts for jobs tend to get filled very quickly, so do not waste time with stale results.

3. Now scroll down through the results for the most relevant posts. Typically, the top few will be actual job posts from the hiring manager which someone in your network has liked/commented or re-posted. Note, this was why having large number of connections helps, as you can use these posts to connect with the decision makers.
   [Note, names of actual people have been hidden, to adhere to privacy concerns.]

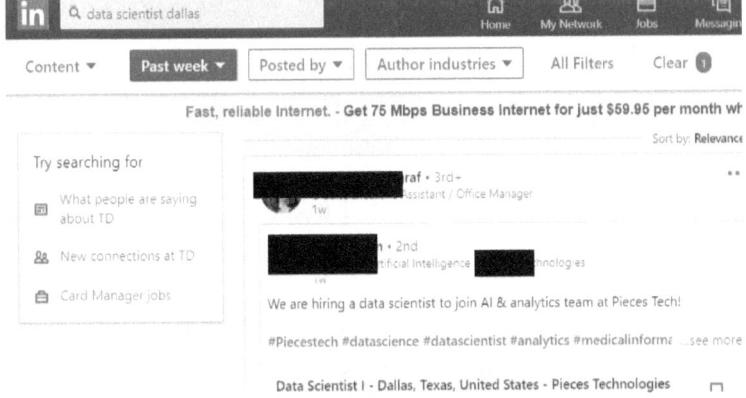

4. In the above image the post was added by one of my 2nd level connections and re-posted by a 3rd

level connection. If I were a candidate interested in this role, I have 3 options:

    a. Like the message. Useful but does not indicate my interest in the role. The hiring manager is not a mind-reader, and most people do not get a notification unless a post reaches 50+ likes.

    b. Comment on the post, saying something along the lines of "interested". This is passive, and I now am forced to wait for the poster to look at my profile, check whether I am a fit and answer back. Some job posters are proactive and will respond, but the wait may be agonizing. This option is also useless if I want to keep my job search a secret.

    c. Best option. Click on the original job poster and send an invitation with the following message template:

"Hi XXX,
Saw your job post for a data scientist at Pieces Tech. Would love to connect and learn how my skills can help your org.
Best wishes, Candidate."

99.999% of LinkedIn users will accept, irrespective of whether they are open networkers or not.

If the contact accepts, but does not respond within 2 days, then look up their email from the LinkedIn profile and send them an email with the sample text below:

"Hello XXX,
Thank you for accepting my LinkedIn
invite to connect.
Saw your job post for the data scientist
position at Pieces Tech. Would love to
learn more and discuss how my skills
might be of use.
Best wishes, Candidate."

Use the same template to send them another LinkedIn message as well.

d. I am not going to provide any follow-up items on this because I have had 100% success rate with this method. This "direct contact" always gets back a response. 95% of the time, the response is to ask for a resume via email or set up an introductory call over the phone. The rest 5% has been feedback to say the role is filled up or I am not a good fit. If you receive the latter, thank the person for their feedback with good grace, and reply that you are ready to help them in the future.

e. In case it so happens, that you do not receive a response via this method (unlikely, but possible) then look up another person from the same company and repeat if you truly love the company.

5. Rinse and repeat for other posts in the original search. Some may have specific constraints such as contractual position only, or a clause saying no F-1 allowed. If the constraint puts you out of the running, then don't message the recruiter to argue the point. For example, if you are not happy with

contract roles, as shown in the image below, then accept it and move on to greener pastures.

6. **Note, this method is highly manual, but it is also why it seems to work with such high accuracy.**

7. Second point to remember is that this search will also show lots of posts you do not care about, as a job-hunting candidate. For example, you may notice posts from recruiters trying to snag a job for the candidates on their books. Skip the post to more relevant ones.

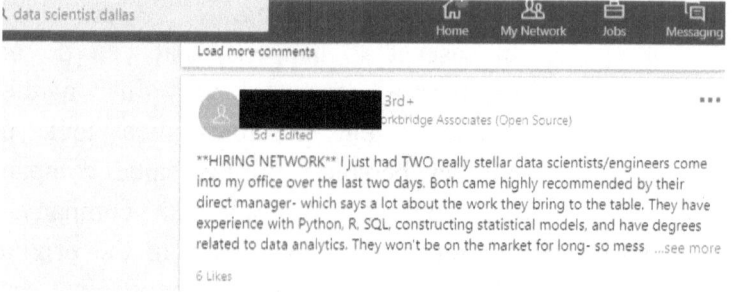

8. Some posts maybe from recruiters with multiple open roles. So, LinkedIn algorithms will combine the "data scientist" and another job with the target

city. Mathematically, correct from a search perspective, but annoying from a job search perspective. Quickly read through and move on.

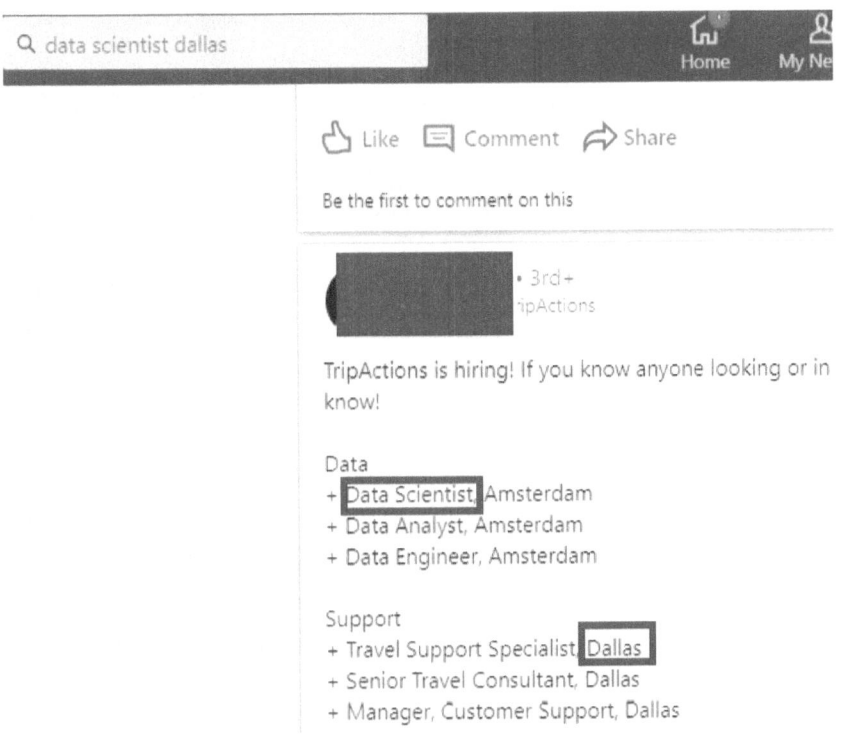

9. Do not ignore posts from recruiters or agencies. They get paid if you do get placed, so it is a win-win for both. They can bypass online application tracking systems and get your resume directly to the hiring manager's desk, so do NOT scoff. Most will also offer valuable tips on how to frame your experience to best advertise you to the manager, advice on interviews, keep you updated on timelines, and basically be your wingman for this process.

10. You will see some repeated roles, and updates from different folks in the same team. Ignore the duplicates. Keeping an Excel tracker to note role, company and contacts will generally help with this issue of duplicates.

6.2 Roles with recruiter names

Now the previous section may have coaxed you to believe that LinkedIn jobs under the "jobs" sections are a complete waste of time. That is only partially true. LinkedIn job postings are useful if the job poster's name is listed. [See image below]

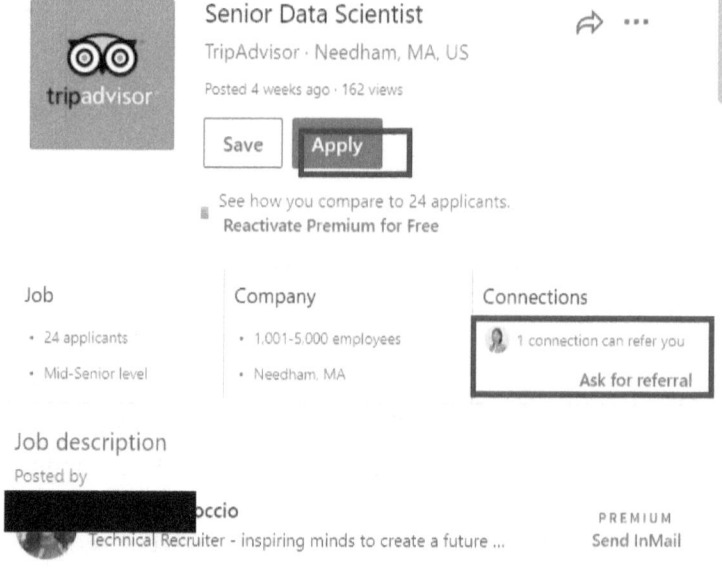

Note, the following:

- "Apply" button indicates that you will NOT be redirected to the company website.
- 1 of my connection works here, so I could ask them for a referral.
- The job poster name and profile are visible.

Here is what you can do:

- If you can see both recruiter name and referral connections, connect directly with job poster first. Like the previous sub-section, invite to the job poster directly, but tweak the message to say that (a) you are interested and have applied to the role, (b) you would love some feedback. Remember to customize your resume when you apply.
- If the job-poster name is missing, but you have connections, then look them up. Do you know them personally? If the answer is yes, email or message them to ask if they will refer you internally. This step will only work if the referral is someone you know from school, college, or previous work. If the contact is someone you only met online, and have never spoken, then please do not make this request. Internal referrals require that this person log in their company intranet, fill your details and put their employee number as referee. Unless they know you, they will not be willing to risk their professional reputation. Saying yes to LinkedIn connections is one thing, but referrals are a big commit. When in doubt, do not do it!

What about job postings with no connections – no referrals or visible job posters? Simple use the company name, job title and go back to the LinkedIn search bar on the home page. Use the earlier method to get a direct connection to the job poster. Again, having a simple Excel tracker helps a lot. Create a list of companies and job roles. Then use them in the search bar and scroll through to get people's names. If you cannot see a similar content post in the first 5 pages, move on to the next role. You can look up a recruiter, using the method in the next section. Once you gather all the names, send messages with slight customizations.

6.3 Connect with recruiters in your target companies

You probably have a list of 10 target companies. If you do not possess such a list, create one.

If you did not find names of job posters in the previous section, then this strategy will help.

Using the search bar on the LinkedIn homepage, type the company name and technical recruiter, and select "People" on the search results.

There are some *boutique recruiting firms* which only specialize in tech jobs and some which only work on filling "Datascience" roles. It is a great idea to connect with such folks. Some will openly tell you that they do not work on entry-level roles but will accept your invitation anyway. In that case, do not despair. These recruiters' LinkedIn feeds might include open roles from others which is a good fit, so connecting with them has zero downside.

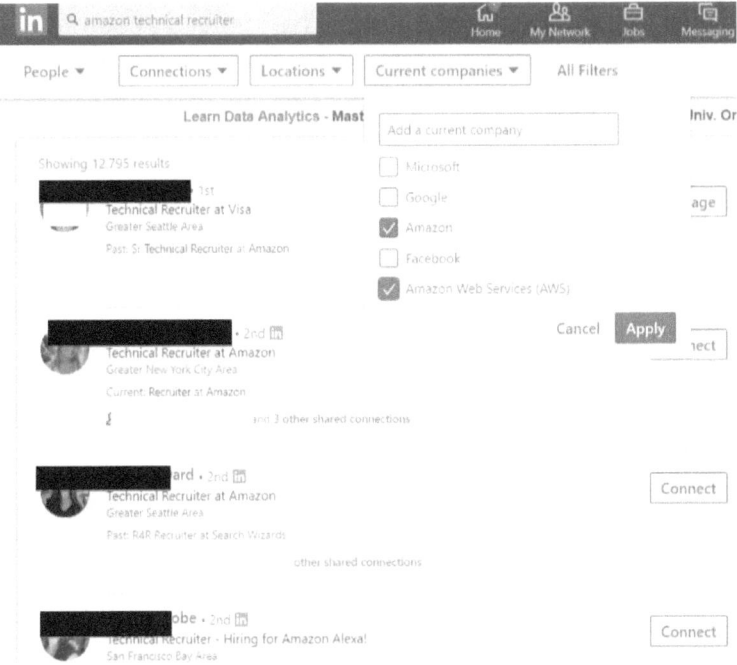

You may need to select "current company", as you may see search results of names who were previously at this company. See the image above, where the first name is a recruiter from Visa, not Amazon.

Message them using the template in the first section.

If you are a student, either current or just graduated, then you can also search with the phrase "<company> campus recruiter".

Warning: I have noticed that LinkedIn will sometimes show me only 2-3 pages of search results and then expects me to upgrade to a paid account to view more results. These many results are generally enough, but if you want to view more, logout and come back after an hour or so. If the problem persists, clear your cache.

6.4 Groups

LinkedIn groups have sadly become quite noisy, with everyone trying to establish their authority or spamming with sales pitches. However, they can be a good resource for job seekers, if you have the patience to scroll through the clutter. You might want to use the "find" command [Ctrl+F] with the phrase "hiring". Somehow adding the job roles seems to make the search invalid.

Note some groups have totally banned job postings. So read through the group rules, which are typically listed on the extreme right of the group homepage.

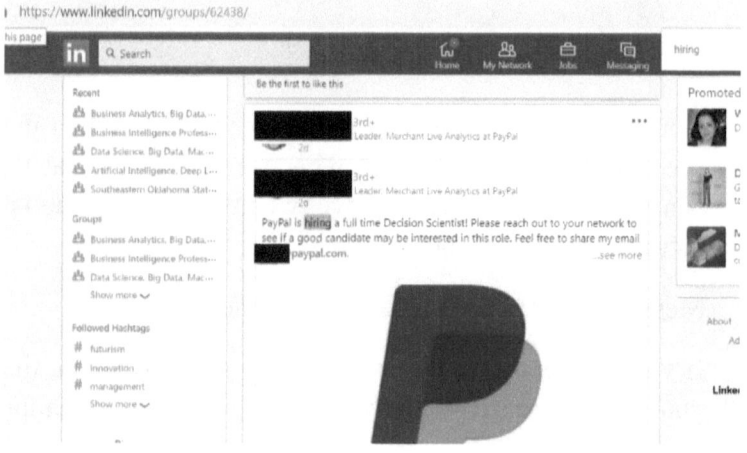

This chapter should have given you enough leads to start looking for relevant jobs. Ideally, you should see 10+ new leads per day.

Short interruption …

Did you like the book so far? If so, please leave a review on Amazon. It will help other jobseekers make progress on their job search to gain the job of their dreams.

If you do not have time to write a long review, feel free to simply state that you found the book useful. You do have the option of editing your review at a future date.

I personally read every email and review, so your feedback will be appreciated to improve this book further.

Thanks, Ann.

P.S.: Simply navigate to Amazon and search "Job Search Strategies for New Grads". Click on the link with this cover. This book might not be the first link, due to sponsored ads. Click on the ***** indicating reviews. You will be taken to a page with a button named "Write a Customer Review".

Ch 7. TWITTER FOR JOB SEARCH

Although Twitter is not as big or popular as LinkedIn, it is still a great resource for job leads. On the plus side, most people rarely use Twitter for job hunting, so there is lesser competition. Plus, there are job aggregator bots that you can follow to receive leads. However, you won't find as many leads as you might on LinkedIn, especially for smaller cities.

In the following sub-sections, you will find strategies to use Twitter to find job leads:

7.1 Twitter search

This is remarkably similar from what you did for LinkedIn. For example, let us look at jobs related to "hiring social media manager Chicago" and hit Enter. On the initial search results, click on "Latest" on the top left, as the default sorting is "top" i.e. tweets with the most engagement (retweets, likes and comments). The search filters are not useful for narrowing down our criteria.

Note, the first is a request for jobs for this person. However, we can see that there are 4 responses. There is nothing preventing you from reaching out to the responders to ask if the role is still open.

You will notice most of the jobs are by job aggregators, but if you scroll down far enough, you will see a couple of job posts by real recruiters and managers.

See image below for another example for project managers in Dallas.

However, please be mindful of the date of the tweet, as the search will often become quite old, depending on the search volume. Another point to note, is that some of these tweets will list roles and companies that you may not know existed on any other job board.

Note, for some cities it is more useful to use "analyst <city>" Try different iterations with titles for your target city, including and excluding the words "hiring", "open roles" and so on.

7.2 Follow recruiter and job-aggregator bots

Specific to entry level and college grad roles, here are my recommendation for job bots on Twitter. These are Twitter accounts that only post jobs related to roles for new grads and young professionals. Many of these roles are quite unique and will not show up in your inbox via LinkedIn or Glassdoor. So, remember to follow these accounts. Sadly, these roles get filled quickly so remember to look frequently and only apply to recent postings.

- @entrylevel_job
- @LewisCareerSvcs
- @joinHandshake

In addition to the above list, do not forget to follow me on Twitter at @anu_analytics, as I do re-tweet interesting datascience jobs that are sent to me or ones that show up on my feed.

For other fields, if you experiment with 10-15 search criteria, you will start to see patterns based on #hashtags, job aggregator names and recruiter names.

Make a private list of these Twitter handles, so you can only look up the latest tweets they post. A private list will help you save time in searching daily and eliminate the odds of new roles getting lost in your massive general Twitter feed.

Ch 8. GIRLBOSS – Networking & Jobs

This site used to be invitation only, but I have found it to be an amazing site – to learn, to get clients and to view job postings. As the name suggests, the site is mainly for women, but there is a large LGBTQ+ group as well.

If you can, do join! I know it feels overwhelming to be on 50 different social media platforms, but this one is valuable.

8.1 Collectives

For recent grads, do subscribe to the following groups, i.e. "Collectives":

- Job Postings
- Freelance Life
- Current Students

There is a group called "Girlboss" but everyone is automatically enrolled, so you do not need to subscribe separately.

Scroll through these groups to check if there are job postings relevant to you. Like Twitter, the feed can get messy, so be sure to scroll until you have read all posts added in the last 2 or 3 weeks.

8.2 Plain Search

Like Twitter, use your expected job title in the search bar and look at related "posts". Due to the way the site is set up, my advice would be to use this search functionality on a desktop only! (not mobile or iPad)

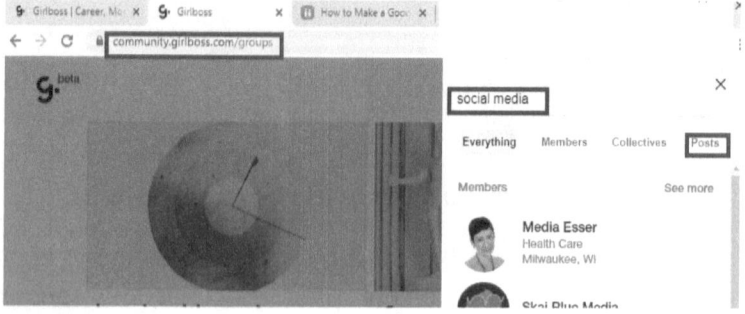

Unfortunately, there is no way to tell how old the posts are from the results section. They are not sorted by date of posting either! [Image below]

Note, that you can see the names of the collectives such roles are posted in. Search for 3-4 titles and make note of all the related collectives. Make sure to subscribe to all of them, so you can view the content in your home feed or by entering that group. This will save you time for scrolling and searching.

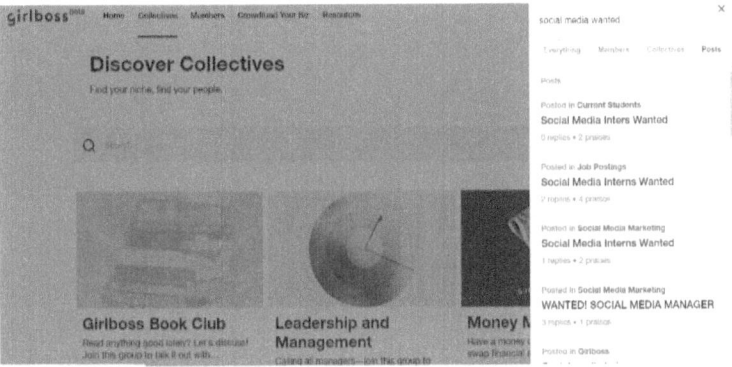

My recommendation is to use the right-click function and open at least the first 15 results using the "open in new tab" option. The date of posting will be listed under the header – ignore anything that is older than 3 weeks shown as "3w".

For the image below, the content is relevant, but the date is not. 43w = 43 weeks ago, so almost zero chance of the role being open!

Social Media

Manhattan & Brooklyn Real Estate Advisor
43w

Can anyone recommend a marketer? I already have a month's worth of content ready to go. I need someone on the backend to engage with people when I cannot thru the day. I hired someone in the past but they only created an algorithm program to like and comment. This only led to un-engaged followers. I'd rather have less followers but be confident in knowing they are consuming my content. Any recs?

8.3 Asking for Work

The members in this community are very engaged and do respond to posts asking for work. Make sure you have a clear title; mention skills you bring to the table and add links to your portfolio if possible.

However, please do not feel entitled and expect responses. You are the one who needs the job, so you will need to approach folks who have already posted.

CH 8. NETWORKING, NETWORKING, NETWORKING!

Except for entry-level positions, networking is still the best way of getting a job quickly, without jumping through a million hoops. However, you must be "smart" about it, and this chapter will tell you how.

8.1 Tell your network

Whether you are a student fresh out of college, or a seasoned professional, we all have networks – our friends, family, co-workers, neighbors, and many more. So here is an easy tip – tell everyone you know that you are looking for a job. Do not be shy, do not be embarrassed, just tell them. But here is the IMPORTANT caveat, tell people what job you want.

Remember the target city and skills you searched in the second and third chapters? Use that knowledge when you are enlisting help. Here is how a typical "ask" would look like:

Hi XXX, I am currently looking for <production assistant> roles, preferably in the <Dallas> area. My target companies are <marketing> firms, but I am open to other domains/companies. If you hear of anything suitable, can you let me know?

Do not feel like you are being desperate or "cheating" or letting people down. Most people are happy to help. I once referred a girl to my manager for a data analyst position, who had not received a single job offer even 2 months after graduation, despite being quite good at coding and communicating skills. She was hired, but here is the thing – she was sent to me for mentoring by someone I respected (let us call him Mr.J), as she was his close friend's daughter. Mr. J sent her to me so I could help her with mock interviews and change her resume to the "hybrid" version. Coincidentally another manager I knew was looking to hire someone on their team, so I referred her, in part to gain brownie points with Mr.J. Networking is weird that way, it works in mysterious ways. Neither the girl's parents, nor the family friend who knew me were in the data science field, Mr.J had no idea that I would be able to refer her.

Similarly, do not scoff at your family or friends who are in fields unrelated to data science or even living across the ocean, that person might be the "bridge" to your potential hiring manager.

If you do not want your current manager to know you are looking, then let your contacts know that as well.

8.2 Meetups

Meetups are a great way of meeting new people and learning new techniques in your field. However, a lot of job seekers, especially students only attend to get job leads. Some even get disrespectful if they meet a hiring manager who is not committing to give them a job. But unless the meetup is for "networking" event for hiring, assume that the relationships you build at meetups are for getting your "second" job, not the first.

Some meetups will advertise hiring events for members, hence make sure you subscribe to such alerts! At the very least add a Google notification alert for this search phrase:

"hiring event <cityname>

8.3 Career Fairs and Hiring Events

Look for technical hiring events in your area. Most large cities have annual events. For example, PhillyTechWeek in Philadelphia has one day dedicated to job fairs. Companies like Deloitte, Accenture, Slalom consulting sometimes have walk-in hiring events in multiple cities. However, you will know it only if you look it up on LinkedIn.

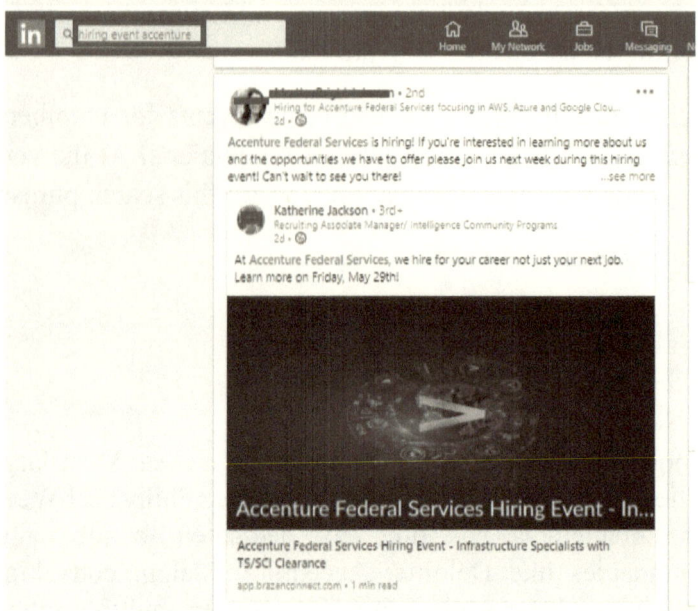

Hiring for Accenture Federal Services focusing in AWS, Azure and Google Clou...
2d

Accenture Federal Services is hiring! If you're interested in learning more about us and the opportunities we have to offer please join us next week during this hiring event! Can't wait to see you there!   ...see more

Katherine Jackson • 3rd+
Recruiting Associate Manager/ Intelligence Community Programs
2d

At Accenture Federal Services, we hire for your career not just your next job.
Learn more on Friday, May 29th!

Accenture Federal Services Hiring Event - In...

Accenture Federal Services Hiring Event - Infrastructure Specialists with TS/SCI Clearance
app.brazenconnect.com • 1 min read

8.4 Other networking opportunities

- Volunteering at local community and hiring events is a fantastic way of meeting potential employer as well as building your brand.
- For students, please do not miss out on any college hiring events, irrespective of what other students say. Some colleges will have different events for different majors, for example business (MBA grads) vs engineering hiring fair. Unless there is a rule against it, attend both.
- Again, if you are a student, then attend "mock interviews" by professionals who visit from large firms. Even if that company is not hiring, you may make an impression, and they could send a reference your way. This has happened to me and

a couple others. At the very least, you will get genuine feedback and can prepare better for the interviews you will attend in the future.

- **For current students:** Attend every campus event by companies, even if you think that they do not hire your major. Believe me, all companies need both technical and business staff. You do not want to miss out on a potential recruiter. In fact, you may overtake the competition because others like you, will opt out under false assumptions. For example, many people assume companies like EY, and Vanguard only hire accounting and business majors. Wrong, they have a huge data-science department that is growing by leaps and bounds. In a similar vein, tech companies often hire liberal arts majors for various roles.

- **Women hiring events:** A lot of companies in larger cities are becoming more aware about increasing women in tech. Hence there are annual events in cities like San Francisco, Philadelphia where companies get together for a job fair targeted solely for women. Some companies also hold events on their company campus, for example JP Morgan Chase (bank) in their Wilmington, DE location. So, if you are a woman looking for a new role, especially after a career break, make sure you RSVP and attend. You may not receive a job at the event, but you will get to meet directly with decision makers who can provide valuable feedback. You might also meet other working women who could potentially refer to a role in their existing company.

8.5 Do not be pushy

This brings us to the next topic, express your need for a job to everyone you know, but do not push them. If people send you leads that seem completely irrelevant (and you will receive such leads), do not get mad. Ignore the lead if you want but thank the person for thinking about you.

8.6 Internships and unpaid projects

Internships and unpaid projects do not pay money; but they can be helpful in other ways:

- You can list it as current employment
- Use the experience to build your portfolio, which is helpful to get future employment.
- Contacts to use if you need recommendations and/or present references.
- If you have been job-searching for a while, it does erode our self-confidence. In such situations, volunteering few hours per week is a good way of getting out of the house and feeling valued.

Finally remember that networking takes time, but the reward of a fabulous job is worth the effort. Also, HR and hiring managers tend to favor folks who come in as referrals and such candidates also benefit from a speedier hiring process.

Ch 9. UPWORK

Upwork, to me personally is a fantastic platform, that lets you earn money, irrespective of your skill level or location. However, I realize that most people see zero results and assume it is lucrative only to contractors in Asian countries.

I have personally used Upwork for ~5 months and made $3000/month on the site, working less than 30 hours per week. It also helped me land my full-time role at Nasdaq! (recruiter came calling, honest story)

Will you earn a $100,000 on Upwork? Highly unlikely, but not impossible if you put in the time, effort and techniques listed below.

9.1 Why choose Upwork?
There are many reasons why you should consider Upwork, but here are the advantages and disadvantages.

9.1.a Advantages

- Start earning money within a week.
- Great way to build your portfolio.
- You can add "freelancer" experience, instead of showing up as "unemployed".
- Wide variety of tasks to suit your skills and expertise.
- You can increase your tax deductions (US), based on local laws.
- You can work at your own pace, fix your own schedule and be your own boss.

- No ceiling on making money.

9.1.b Disadvantages

- You do have to bid on jobs, which takes time. When you initially start, it might feel like no one is ready to give you a chance, just like no one is willing to hire. Initially, it will feel like you are overworked and underpaid.
- Upwork takes a 20% commission, from every gig, until you earn $500 from that client. To me, this feels like being looted, but sadly, you do need to pay the marketplace for bringing you a wide variety of gigs. Plus, you as a freelancer, get peace of mind since Upwork guarantees payment and will help you with disputes, if any.
- In the US, you need to pay quarterly taxes as a freelancer and fill out Schedule C (more paperwork) when you file your annual taxes. Some states (like Delaware) you will also require a general business license, even if you don't plan to open an LLC. On the other hand, the paperwork is useful during employment verification.

9.2 Getting Started on Upwork

9.2.a Fill Your Profile

- Fill out your complete profile, like LinkedIn. Upload summary documents of your portfolio. Link to your portfolio (if applicable) and website (if any) and LinkedIn.
- If you are in the US, do not keep your hourly rate below $20. Change accordingly for other countries. Keeping it artificially low makes you

look desperate and good clients will wonder about the quality of work you will deliver at such ridiculous low rates. Please do not worry what potential clients will think, as the ones who want entry level work are going to pick the lowest possible number, which is beyond your control. Clients who care about getting their work done, will be happy to discuss your rate, if they like the rest of your profile.

- The way you look for jobs will be different for your first 5 gigs, versus later.

9.2.b Looking for Gigs

- Whenever you look for jobs, make sure you do not look at entry level jobs as you do not have any control over others who can underprice you.
- Do not despair over the fact, that long term hourly jobs at $50 do not exist. Your main priority is to get some work, to attract full time work, while earning money. Think of this as "pin money" to sponsor your job search.
- Hourly jobs are good. Mainly, because you can often get tasks for $20 that a good programmer can finish in 30 mins. Or a $100 project that can completed in less than 4 hours.
- Irrespective of how long you are on Upwork, you will custom reply to every gig. If you like, keep a template but customize it before hitting send. Yes, each one.
- Avoid jobs where the "hired" stat = 1. It usually means the job has been assigned, but the formalities are incomplete. No point bidding for a lost opportunity.

- Read the full job description. Some posters add special requests (like 2-hour turnaround) or local candidate requirements that might be impossible to fulfill. Some add a phrase that needs to be the first line of your message. You will be astonished how many freelancers make such avoidable mistakes.

- Sometimes you will have questions, too or a suggestion to make the project better. Put those in the reply, the client will feel happy to get a trusted and proactive consultant. If the project description is bare bones, then offer to talk about it in detail for a free 30 mins consultation. Any less than 30 mins, and you cannot get enough details, anything more and you waste "billable" time.

- For every job, think through how you will tackle the task. In your bid, add the task steps and deliverables, and if possible, a sample from other similar projects. This takes longer, but you are more likely to impress the client and get hired. For example, imagine the job description says, "survey analysis" and some generic details about the number of variables and types of questions. In your response, you can mention that you will be analyzing in R and will provide (a) summary doc in word, with insights and p-values, (b) the r program code as a textbook file, so the results can be replicated. Attach a sample report from other survey analysis with analysis on 4 variables, and maybe one moderator variable. If you have never done such an analysis, try one for practice using a free dataset from Kaggle.com or the Stack overflow developer survey or something from the bls.gov site. Then attach to your response.

- Do not hound the Clients! The employers on Upwork are typically busy entrepreneurs with limited staff and budget. If not, they would have a full-time employee working on the task. Give them a week at least to get back, and if they do not respond, then assume they hired someone else. And MOVE ON with your life.
- A hit rate of 20%-30% is normal and anything above 50% is extraordinary. By hit rate I mean, that I get hired for 2 gigs, for every 10 that I apply.
- Once you have completed 50 hours on Upwork, you can start to pick and choose what jobs you bid. At this point, you will want to get jobs that pay you at least $20-$30 per hour, so estimate the work before you bid. If you can get more, even better as this estimation will cover the hours you spend on bidding, creating proposals, etc. The more work you receive, the higher you can bid. I know freelancers who charge $1000 per project and reject invitations to anything else.
- Remember the more work you get, the higher you will rank on the site, and show up for employers who post projects. Yes, clients do get recommendations on profiles and can choose to invite such folks to bid.
- Make sure you add some of these projects in your Upwork profile, LinkedIn profile and personal website. It will help you rise in local searches on LinkedIn, too.

9.2.c Your first 5 gigs:

- The first 5 jobs are tasks you will take on to get testimonials on the site, and to show you have done some work. So, the rate does not matter.
- Tags like "rising talent" and Upwork stats only show up 90 days after you join, so you are going to mention you are new to the site in every bid.
- If you like, specify that you have listed a low rate as you want to get a high rating on the site. Clients will be happy to hire an excellent professional, that too, at a discount.
- Over-deliver. It stands to reason that you are going to complete the work before time. Thank the employer for their job, remind them to provide feedback, and ask to be considered in case any work comes up in the future.

9.2.d Pricing

You can edit the hourly or project rate, irrespective of the rate on your profile. Use the client reviews to get a sense of how much the client typically pays for similar jobs. Also look at the price ceiling for the current job. I typically take 10% off, so the clients feel they are paying less than what they budgeted. Do not discount any further, as you do not want to leave too much money on the table.

9.3 Once you get hired.

- Use the time tracker on the site to record your work, irrespective of whether it is an hourly job or prepaid project. This will discipline you to focus (no browsing the internet during work!) and help you gauge how much time projects truly take. This will help you bid better for future projects. Plus, the evidence is useful should you ever need to dispute a case with a rogue client.

- Keep the client updated on your progress every 3 days at a minimum.
- Let the client know if there are any delays or if the data shows something you had not expected when you accepted the project. Do not whine to the client, but come up with a solution as well, such as extension of the deadline, or changes to the contract. If they accept, good for you. If not, treat this as a learning opportunity and be more mindful if you need to discuss projects in more detail, for future projects.
- Give feedback to the client, with their name. This will help other freelancers, share some good karma!

In conclusion, a well-crafted response with laid out process and deliverables, a reasonable (but not ridiculously low bid) and samples will increase the client's confidence in you and want them to hire you.

Ch 10. GOOD OLD MANUAL SEARCH

This chapter lists a couple of miscellaneous tactics that can help you get a job.

10.1 Startups in your area

Most job seekers want to join big name companies because of the fat paychecks and security they represent. Therefore, they fail to realize that startups and small companies are more work, but you also learn skills to boost your career. Plus, startups often have a shorter hiring cycle, which means you can start earning faster. Not to mention it is easiest to get a job when you do not need one.

You can locate these companies using the following techniques:

10.1.a Simple Google search.

Look for articles in local online news websites listing the previous year's fast-growing startups. For example, a Google search for "Chicago startups":

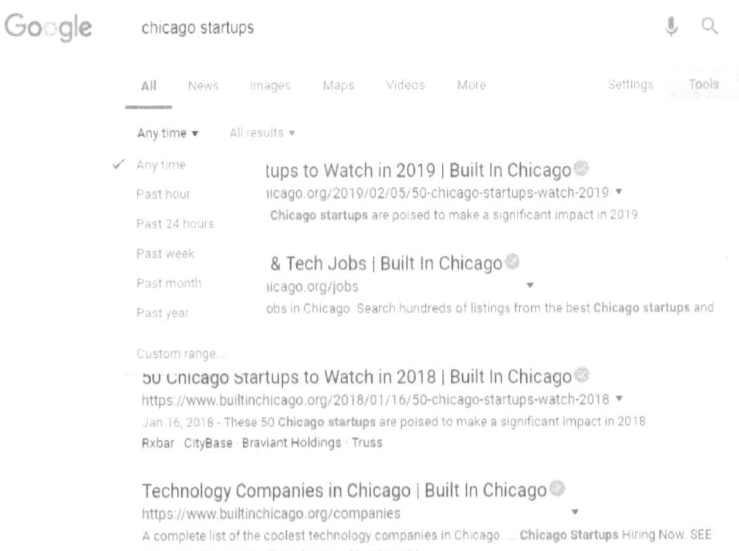

Filter by "past month" and you will see lists of top 10 companies, or local companies that are expanding furiously. "builtinchicago.com" is a site that keeps track of local companies and has a job board, too.

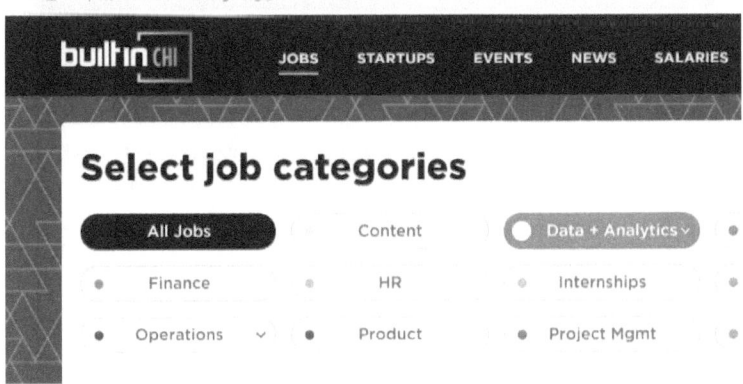

Local newspapers (digital) will have listings of local jobs, that would not normally be advertised on larger job boards. For example, technical.ly is an online website that hosts networking meetups and job postings local to extremely specific cities (DC, Philadelphia, Baltimore, etc.) This article in Americaninno.com lists the hottest startups local to Chicago. There are similar sites and articles for most of the larger cities in the US, and abroad.

10. 2 Chamber of commerce

Scour through the local chamber of commerce website to locate employers in your area, narrow by interest, then look up their websites. Smaller companies often post the names and contact details of hiring managers, so you may even be able to cold-email the managers directly. You have nothing to lose, and everything to gain.

10.3 Educational institutions

Do not forget local colleges and institutions. You will have to apply online, but most job aggregators (like indeed.com or glassdoor.com) will not have these listings, so you may be able to notice a job that others do not know about. On the other hand, most colleges only post data analyst or reporting analyst type positions.

10.4 Niche job boards

Please look at niche job boards, specializing solely on your roles. For example, if you are a writer, these sites will help:

- Freedom with Writing
- ProBlogger
- Technical.ly Jobs – This site only caters to the US East Coast in the mid-Atlantic area, primarily Philadelphia, Baltimore, Brooklyn/NYC, Delaware, and Washington D.C. But it covers both tech and non-tech roles.
- Inc.com – this is not limited to data science roles, but it does give a list of employers that you might otherwise have ignored.
- Reddit – Most users ignore it from a jobseeker perspective, but there are dedicated sub-sections only listing jobs. I would suggest using the site to scour jobs and then using the techniques listed on the LinkedIn section to make personal connections and reach out to hiring managers.

Again, I repeat, do not blithely apply on these site. Instead check if there are jobs you like, and which match your skills. Next, use LinkedIn to connect with the recruiters working at these firms and express your interest.

SECTION D – INTERVIEW PREP

Ch 11. INTERVIEW PROCESS

The interview process will vary from company to company, but the most common format is as follows:

HR introductory phone call -> Hiring manager phone call -> Technical interview -> Onsite interview with manager and peers -> Salary negotiation -> Offer

With advances in technology, the format of the interview might vary. Some use Skype calls, some employers send take home tests for technical interviews, some use software for real-time coding evaluation or a combination of all the above. The sections below give a short overview along with dos and don'ts for each format.

11.1 HR/ introductory call

This will be a short call from a recruiter or HR manager and typically lasts 15-30 minutes. The main purpose of this call is to get a brief overview of your work experience and ensure there are no serious red flags in your resume. Usually if you are not a good fit, they will let you know immediately. Otherwise, the call will normally end with the HR tell you that they will forward your resume to the hiring decision-maker.

80% of the time this will be followed by an email scheduling time for a short call with the hiring manager. The rest 20% the hiring manager may decide to go with an internal referral or decide they want somebody with more experience or a different skillset. The HR should ideally let you know either way, but if you do not hear back within a week it is perfectly acceptable to send a follow-up email. If you still do not hear back after 2 weeks, then assume the job went to someone else and move on.

If you have had a break in your career, do use this call to point it out and explain it away in 2-3 sentences. For example, you might say that you took a break to care for a parent but now you have hired a fulltime nurse and therefore are free to get back to the workforce. Moreover, you have refreshed your skills and added new ones so you will be able to hit the ground running.

11.1.a New moms
Be honest. Most employers understand caring for a newborn is hard work. In the US, this can also be quite expensive with daycare costs in larger cities and often the mother is the one to leave her career. So be truthful but strategic. For example, my sister mentioned how she had designed her own website and grown a personal blog to 500+ subscribers with $0 marketing, during her 5-year career break. While not relevant directly to data science it did highlight her ambition, keen business acumen and coding skills. She also mentioned the certifications she had completed with flying colors and was able to receive a fabulous job offer that was 100% remote with excellent pay.

11.1.b Cautionary tale
If you have had more than 50 introductory calls but less than 5 interviews with the hiring manager, then this is a red flag for your profile. This is rare but does happen if your resume looks flaky (read lying on your resume) or if

you resume looks like a job-hopper (3+ jobs staying less than 8 months per role). You may also want to look if you are applying for roles where you are considered under-qualified or over-qualified. In that case, refer to Section C (chapters 4 and 5) and apply more strategically. If possible, ask a well-wisher to conduct a mock interview and see if you are making any obvious mistakes while presenting your skills.

11.2 Hiring manager call

This will also be ~30 minutes call where the manager will tell you the basics about the role and get a sense of your work experience. If you do not make any glaring mistakes you will move on to the next stage, if you do the following:

- Truly listen to the manager and understand his expectations from this role. This is the person who might control your career, so it benefits you to listen carefully.
- Based on the description, present a short spiel about how you can fulfill all those duties. Keep it short but give examples of academic or work projects that translate well to this role. If you read the job description you should be able to answer this well.
- Do not tell the manager that you are the BEST candidate since you have no clue who else is interviewing for this role. However, you do have to sell how you are a GREAT candidate who meets all the checkboxes in terms of technical and soft skills. You cannot force the manager to

hire you, but you can make it hard to find a reason to reject you.

11.2.a What to ask the interviewer?

The manager will give you time to ask Qs. My favorite questions are listed below:

- What is the biggest priority in this role?
- What kinds of technical and soft skills would help a candidate excel in this role?
- What is the one thing you love the most in this role, and one thing you dislike in this role?
- Assume you hired me or someone else in this role, and at the end of the year you gave that person a full 5on5 rating. What would that person have accomplished to get this rating?
- Most hiring managers are pleasantly surprised with these questions and happy to go into details. A few admit they have not really thought about it but proceed to answer. In all cases, you have shown the manager that you really are thinking about the role and adding value to the company, not just going through the motions to get any random high-paying job.
- Once they finish answering, thank them for the insight and quickly use some of their points to reiterate how your skills and experience can help this manager accomplish their goals.
- If the manager must leave early or does not have time to let you ask questions, quickly mention that you do have questions and will email it to HR to pass it on to him. I say HR, as you rarely

get the email address of the hiring manager. If you do have it offer to email it to this manager, so she can answer in leisure.

11.3 Interview Logistics & Tips

For the call with hiring manager and/or HR, make sure you will be in a quiet place without any interruptions. Do NOT take the call in your current employer's phone booth rooms, a washroom (foolish but has happened to me personally) or on the train on your way home. Some companies do monitor conference rooms so you might be severely penalized for it. Take a sick day or check if you can work from home. In the US, public libraries have meeting rooms that can be booked in advance.

The first 2 minutes of both calls should be used to check if the audio connection is appropriate for both parties. If this is not the case, reschedule on a later date.

Occasionally, there will be personal emergencies causing you to reschedule. If you give the HR/manager more than 2 hours' cancellation notice with a very valid reason, things will be fine. If you do need to cancel apologize profusely as they are taking time out of your busy schedule to accommodate you and now need to do it again.

11.4 Technical interviews

For some roles these are unavoidable. Or if you have put programming and software skills on your resume, you will be grilled about it.

With new software available, technical interviews can be in-person, via video conference or even collaborative. Some popular methods are listed below:

11.4.a White board

This is rare but does happen in some onsite interviews. You will be given a problem and expected to code the solution on a white board. Remember to ask questions to understand the problem, explain the logic, which programming language you selected and talk through the code you are writing.

For most of us, writing code without an IDE editor and without looking snippets on Google is hard, so you will need to practice. Writing code on a white board in front of an audience is harder, so make sure you brush up on concepts. If needed look at the book "Cracking the coding interview".

11.4.b Take home tests

This is the most common scenario for data analyst and data scientist roles. You will have a deadline and most HR contacts will specify when the test question becomes available.

Dos and Don'ts:

- As soon as you get the email, open the attachment and check whether you can open the document/ link/ pdf. If you are sent a Dropbox link, make sure you are able to download a copy. This seems like common sense, but I have seen candidates who received the link on Friday afternoon and only opened it on Sunday night to realize that the link was broken or valid only for 24 hours. HR can enable the link again, but this reflects badly on the candidate since we know they are not serious about this position.

- Use the full available time. Most exams state how much time they will take, but you might be different. The earlier you start, the more time you must polish things up. Remember you do not need to say you spent the whole week doing the assignment.

- Irrespective of whether a summary document is asked or not, provide one. Data analysis is just one part of the role. Cleaning messy data, exploring it and providing final recommendations for action are equally important parts. Show your employer how you can decipher meaningful insights and present them in a concise and compelling way.

- If you are getting a chance to present this code in a scheduled onsite interview, then this summary doc will be helpful to build a ppt doc and an outline for your talk.

11.4.c Code walk-through

For entry level roles, managers may ask you to present a project of your choice and walk them through the code. This feels scary but we only want to check whether you have basic analytics competency. Allowing the candidate to choose the project is meant to make the session less stressful.

- If you can, present something unique.
- If possible, present something that is relevant to the company you are interviewing with. For my

interview with Nasdaq I created an interactive Tableau-style dashboard using R presenting stock price movements for the largest companies in their proprietary QQQ portfolio. For a media company, I tracked and pulled Twitter follower counts (using Twitter API) and showed how recent viral articles caused their follower counts to spike and ebb. This takes extra effort, but it will help you stand out immensely.

- Practice. Present to a friend or senior family member and prepare for possible questions.

11.4.d Collaborative editor

These are gaining in popularity, but they do feel stressful even for senior developers. The concept is that you will be writing code in a video call with screenshare, and the interviewer can see what you are doing.

Depending on the software you may or may not be able to use Google or Stack overflow. Having someone virtually watch over your shoulder does feel weird, but you may not have an option.

Typically, not used for entry-level roles, but I am seeing these interviews become standard for experienced data scientist hires.

11.4.e Online coding exams

If the role entails SQL and/or Python, then you may be sent a link to give a coding exam. These are normally timed exams. From my personal experience, most of these are medium to easy, if the candidate does not get stuck on a question. The editor generally does not auto complete, and you cannot test your code, which is a major handicap to most interviewees.

Again, practice in Notepad and then run the code in IDE to get better with your coding skills.

11.5 Case Study Analysis

This will be a part of the interview process only for consulting companies or for roles with high visibility. The "Vault" guide is an old book from 2007, but the concepts are still valid. Download and store as another technique in your arsenal. You can either Google it, or download it from this link.

11.6 Onsite interviews

If you made it to the onsite office interview stage, congratulations! You are much closer than the rest of the competition. If the hiring manager finds you reasonably competent and you do not make any glaring mistakes, you have a good chance of getting hired.

Onsite interviews last between 3 hours to a full day and the objective is to evaluate the candidate by multiple interviewers. One will be the manager or his peer, one interview with a senior manager, one with someone outside the group (for objectivity) and one optionally with folks who are peers or junior to the role. An interview with HR (again) is also possible.

Dos and Don'ts:

- You may get asked to walk through your resume again and again. Do not get annoyed or impatient. Display courtesy and grace for all the interviews.
- You may get asked the same behavioral question repeated by every interviewer. It might be coincidence or a shrewd tactic to see if you keep changing answers.
- It is perfectly acceptable to ask questions in return. Read section 11.2 for sample questions.

11.6.a Stress test

You may be faced with 2 or more interviewers where they fire questions at you and give extraordinarily little time to answer. This is common for cross-functional roles and in consulting companies, to evaluate how you fare under pressure.

Be cool and answer patiently.

11.6.b Panel interview

Multiple interviewers, single candidate. The questions will not seem as interrogative as a stress interview but being alone with so many senior folks can be intimidating. This type of interview includes panel presentation and technical interviews.

11.6.c Lunch interview

Treat this the same as an interview in an office.

Dos and Don'ts:

- Do not order items that will be difficult or messy to eat. This is still an interview and you do not want to talk with your mouth full.
- Do not order alcohol, even if the interview asks or orders one for themselves. [I should not even need to mention this, but I have seen candidates make this mistake repeatedly.]
- Be respectful.
- Feel free to ask the interviewer (or a team) questions about his role, what they enjoy about the company, culture, etc.
- Do not ask about compensation, educational reimbursement, or any other type of compensation.
- Do not talk politics or religion unless the interviewer broaches those topics.

11.7 Skype interview/ Video conference

Alternatives to onsite and phone interviews. With the pandemic, these are becoming quite popular and will likely remain so as cost-cutting measures in the future.

Dos and Don'ts:

- Make sure you are dressed well and in a clean room with good lighting.
- Ideal would be to have a large blank wall behind you.
- If you are taking the video call in your home, lock the door to ensure no one accidentally walks in or disturbs you.
- If the HR accepts, offer to connect 15 minutes prior to the call to test the connection. I once had

an interview where the video in their office was extremely grainy. I could see them, but they could not, so everything had to be moved back by an hour until their tech support fixed the issue. Unfortunately, this meant I had to be on call for most of the extra hour, so the technician could ensure my video was coming through.

- If you have back-to-back video conferences, then ensure that the interviewer does not cut the connection. Ask each new interviewer if they can see and hear you without difficulty.

Now that you have understood the different types of interviews, let us dive into the next chapter with real-life questions.

Ch 12. BEHAVIORAL INTERVIEW QUESTIONS

You optimized your profile, you connected with managers and now you have an interview call with a good company. Here is a list of 25+ interview questions to help you prepare for those meetings. The questions below are sorted logically into sections, although some questions can fall into multiple sections.

12.1 Qs to judge your passion and interest.

These will be questions to judge whether you are really interested in the company and role or whether you just want "a" job for the money. At entry level positions, it does not matter a whole lot, still these questions do help to eliminate candidates who are going to leave before the year is out or if there are any obvious red flags.

On the positive side, if you do interview well and demonstrate a sincere passion for the job, it will create an extremely favorable impression since the expectations from new grads is typically set to an exceptionally low bar.

1. **Tell me about yourself.**

   Most interviewers use this as an icebreaker and to see how well you communicate. So please do not use it as an excuse to ramble on your life story. A great answer would quickly describe your experiences up to this point, explain why you are a fit. If possible, you should (optional) throw in a memorable trivia about you so the interview has a clear memory hook to remember you among all the interviewees he meets for that role.

IMPORTANT REMINDER – Every interview question should be answered with one main goal: how do you show that you will add value to the manager and his team? Prepare for every question to show how the employer benefits from hiring you, not what you expect to gain.

2. **Why are you interested in this role/ company/ industry?**
   If you do not have a technical background, then this is just to gauge whether you are genuinely interested or simply here for the money, and therefore liable to quit if things get hectic.

3. **Describe how you overcame a challenge in your work.**
   For any behavioral question, use the STAR technique to present your answer.
   S – Situation. Short background
   T – Task. What was the goal?
   A – Action. What steps did you take?
   R – Results. What happened at the end, because of your action? Ideally the results should **always** reflect positively on you, but if you do decide to use a neutral story, do add comments to say what you learnt from the situation and how it has helped you in later situations.

4. **How do you approach a project?**
   This is basically to check your logical thinking abilities and to gauge whether you can work without supervision and constant handholding.

5. **What do you do for fun?**
   This sounds like an icebreaker question, but this question is also used to gauge whether you are a cultural fit. Unless the company is a liberal startup or known for an extremely casual atmosphere, please keep your answers conservative. Do your homework on the company and try to make sure that you fit the persona of an ideal company. Disclaimer – this is not an invitation to lie, please do NOT do that. If you truly think you are not a cultural fit, then treat the interview experience as an experiment and reflect seriously whether you would want to work in that company, should you be offered the role.
   For techie roles, it is perfectly acceptable to be "geeky" and talk about a pet software project you are building.

6. **Pick up a project from your resume/GitHub which had a great impact. OR tell me about an interesting data science project.**
   If you read the initial chapters, then you should have some interesting projects on hand to talk about. Even entry-level data analysts can get asked this question, so be prepared. You do not need a super original idea, but you do need to present your unique take on the subject. The expectation is that you show (1) you can write decent code which is well-documented. (2) you

know how to present your findings and have acceptable communication skills.

7. **Being from electrical/economic/bioscience background, why do you want to join as a data analyst?**
Similar expectations as Q2.

8. **Why are you looking for a new job?**
"I am unemployed/ broke/ desperate/hate my current employer / hate my current manager." are all wrong answers. Even if you are in this situation, you do not need to vent it to your future manager. If you are a student or parent returning to the workforce, be honest. Otherwise say something neutral along the lines of 'looking for new growth opportunities.

If a recruiter reached out on LinkedIn, say truthfully that you are not actively looking, but you found this specific job listing interesting.

If you have had multiple jobs in the last 4 years, be aware that the hiring manager is trying to judge if you are a "job hopper". Millennials have received this unnecessary stereotype, so there may be an unconscious bias at play. In such cases it is acceptable to say that you are not actively looking, just answering specific roles. Then explain how the job fits your experiences and how you can add value.

9. **How do you find out trending queries/topics? Finding if you take initiative and keep your skills/knowledge updated.**

Each person will answer differently, but some decent answers include Coursera, Udemy, Forbes magazines, Wall street journal and relevant websites. Technology and globalization are evolving rapidly, so you must have an acceptable answer. Do not state you are so busy that you have not had time to keep updated with new skills.

10. **Are you a team player or an individual contributor?**
The correct answer is both, irrespective of what the role entails. You need to be self-motivated to do your tasks well and within deadlines. Yet, no team works in a silo, so you do need to have good team skills.

11. **Where do you see yourself in 5 years?**
There are no correct answers for this Q, but there are some horribly wrong ones! Do not say "CEO" (unrealistic) or state that you want to open your own company; no one wants to train the next competitor! Ideally, you should state that you see yourself in a place that aligns with roles 1 or 2 promotions above the job you are interviewing for. Feel free to expand accordingly. Or, if your research has shown you some interesting groups inside the company, say that you might want to move into that group after 3 years to broaden your expertise.
Do NOT downplay the current role!

12.2 Product Companies - Facebook, LinkedIn, Uber

If you are interviewing for product-based companies like Facebook, Uber, Shopify or even banking companies, then please do a thorough research on what the company does, its products, new and recent launches, latest company news, changes in the executive team, and so on. It is a BAD idea to be ignorant about the company and ask these when the interview gives you time to pose questions back.

12. Metrics to measure success/failure of one Facebook product.

This question is used to assess your logical thinking and your familiarity with the products. Use that knowledge to pose some basic metrics (product downloads, increase in per customer LTV, reduction in churn, etc.) and KPIs, basic A/B testing and KPI monitoring.

13. Suppose FB wants to launch feature X on product Y - how would you assess whether this is a good idea? How about when standard AB Testing does not work?

Similar to above.

14. What do you think are Deliveroo/ GrubHub/ Stripe's biggest costs?

If you studied the company well, you should be able to make an educated guess. State your answer along with your logic. If necessary, the interviewer can correct you.

Your answer will reveal whether you are able to look beyond basics or obvious choices and grasp what is truly vital to the company.

15. Would you rather take on a more technical role, or focus on business problems? What would your ideal project be like?

The perfect answer will depend on the job description, and from the role description the manager provided (if any). Ideally you would say you are good in both roles, and then choose the side that matches the description. If you are interviewing for a role that is the opposite to what you secretly prefer, reflect if you will really be happy in the role.

16. How would you measure the health of Mentions, Facebook's app for celebrities?

How can FB determine if it is worth it to keep using it? If a celebrity starts to use Mentions and begins interacting with their fans more, what part of the increase can be attributed to a celebrity using Mentions, and what part is just a celebrity wanting to get more involved in fan engagement?

Like Q12 and 13 of this section.

17. How would you prioritize which country to expand Slack to for furthering the International effort?

To answer this Q, you will need to know which the current markets are for the company and choose an emerging market (South America or China or smaller tech hubs in Europe). Explain why you chose the answer. Note, the company already has a base in India.

18. **Lyft/ Uber - What are the different factors that could influence a rise in average wait time of a driver?**

Business acumen matters in all roles. These types of questions also show that you have researched about the industry and the company, and are truly committed to helping the company grow.

19. **What would you improve with the Uber/ LinkedIn/ Candy crush app?**

This question tests both your familiarity with the product and your business acumen. Unless you are a loyal user, you will not really be able to answer this question.

20. **You have been tasked with creating a marketing campaign for our Nike shoe product for cyclists. What will your approach be?**

These will obviously be for marketing or sales roles. Typically, students may not get such questions, but you never know! Such questions are designed to evaluate whether the candidate understands the company's work or not.

12.3 Software Skills

If you have any software listed in your resume or if the job description asked for prerequisites, then do expect to be grilled on it.

12.4 Company Qs

Sites like Glassdoor have a huge library of interview questions. Check all the questions related to (a) the company you are interviewing at, (b) the job title you are interviewing at.

Research answers for at least the first 50 Qs in each category. You will notice the next few start are often variations of the first 50.

Ch 13. SOME MORE ADVICE...

The techniques listed in this book will help you find a data science job quickly. Job-hunting is a fulltime job and can be quite demotivating. Believe in yourself, do not let your coding skills get rusty.

At the same time, do not be too demanding. Competition for data science jobs is fierce, especially at the lower levels. At first, if you fail to get a job in your dream company, don't fret. You can switch in 6-8 months. Again, it is easiest to get a job when you already have one. (as quoted by dozens of recruiters and hiring managers). Do not foolishly reject a $4,000 job and waste months in the hopes of getting a $10,000 job that may or may not materialize. The techniques in this book will help you even if you already have a job, so you can continue looking outside office hours.

Thank you for reading this book and wish you the absolute best in your job search!

[Don't forget to leave a review on Amazon – your feedback is extremely important to me!]

CH 14. ALL BONUS CONTENT HERE

14.1 New Niche Sites

Some recent alternatives to job search platforms are:

- Keyvalues.com – This site mostly has startups and companies in growth phase, but I did see a lot of remote positions. They also have some interesting product companies which claim to be 100% family friendly, meaning if you need to attend a function at your child's school, you can. For some people, values are as important as salary and this site will help those that do.
- WorkataStartup – This site is the hiring portal for companies associated with YC Combinator, a world-renowned startup incubator. Most of the jobs relate to software engineering or sales, but I did see a couple of data scientist and data engineer roles, too. It is more of a matching engine between companies and applicants, and the roles are mandatorily at small growing companies. Plus, you receive the opportunity to work at a startup which may have the potential to become the next Uber or Airbnb.
- AngelList – Noticed I had not included this site for startup jobs. I used it couple years ago, and mostly saw CTO/biz dev and software roles, and very few datascience roles. However, that has changed a lot and now the site has multiple jobs for data analyst/ manager/ scientist. I saw roles from India, US, LatAm and many where the role allows 100% remote work.
- TripleByte – tech roles

About the Author

Anupama Rajaram (aka Ann) is award-winning technology professional with 8+ years' experience working with Financial giants like NASDAQ, TD bank and BlackRock. She currently handles risk management for the credit card portfolio for a large US bank.

She lives with her family in Delaware, USA and enjoys traveling, reading and blogging on her website www.journeyofanalytics.com She is passionate about promoting women in STEM, including mentoring young women for professional programs. She also leads a 1500+ tech meetup group to foster collaboration and new learning.

For more career advice, follow her on Medium.com at https://medium.com/@anupamaprv or LinkedIn at anupamaprv

One Last Thing...

If you enjoyed this book or found it useful, I would really appreciate if you could post a short review on Amazon. Your feedback really does make a difference and can help others land their dream job in the exciting field of data science. I personally read all the reviews so your honest opinion will make this book even better.

Thanks again for your support!